THE KILLERS

DESTINY IS
CALLING ME

THE KILLERS

DESTINY IS
CALLING ME

JARRET KEENE

MANIC D PRESS
SAN FRANCISCO

Design: Roger Erik Tinch
ISBN 1-933149-10-8

While this book is neither authorized nor endorsed by the band, we
sincerely hope they find it entertaining or at least mildly amusing.

Library of Congress Cataloging-in-Publication Data

Keene, Jarret, 1973-
  The Killers : destiny is calling me / Jarret Keene.
      p. cm.
  ISBN-13: 978-1-933149-10-3 (trade pbk. original)
  1. Killers (Rock group) 2. Rock musicians--Nevada--Las Vegas. I.
Title.
  ML421.K49K44 2006
  782.42166092'2--dc22

                              2006007853

CONTENTS

Bass, electronic drums, keys,
strings. Ages 18-33 pref. Influences:
Radiohead, Bjork, Beatles, Foo
Fighters. ▓▓▓▓▓▓▓▓▓▓▓
▓▓▓▓▓▓▓▓

BASS PLAYER NEEDED- Drowning

It started out with a kiss,

how did it end up like this?

It was only a kiss.

It was only a kiss.

—from the Killers' hit single "Mr. Brightside"

Icehouse Lounge, Las Vegas, June 2004

WHAT'S ALL THE *FUSS*?

THE KILLERS | DESTINY IS CALLING ME

The Killers: Destiny Is Calling Me peels back the glam and exposes the grit behind the band that emerged from the cultural desert of Las Vegas to become the top modern rock act of 2005. Indeed, the Killers' three-year rise to international fame and Grammy-nominated acclaim was full of blood, sweat and tears, most of which were spent in the dingiest rehearsal spaces and dive bars in Sin City. From the most lurid drag-queen nightclubs to soundproof rehearsal rooms on the university campus, Brandon Flowers and Co. have seen and done it all with a powerful work ethic that most fans have yet to recognize, much less understand.

WHO ARE THESE PEOPLE?

Brandon Richard Flowers

was born June 21, 1981 in Las Vegas, Nevada. He grew up in Mormon-saturated Nephi, Utah. In Nephi, he was the only Smiths fan and never had a girlfriend while he lived there, since Nephi was a little farm town of just 2,000 people where football was everything. He played golf and listened to Elton John. He had four sisters who instilled in him the importance of always having great hair.

His parents made him take piano lessons, but the person responsible for Brandon's musical education was his older brother, who showed him Smiths videos and U2's *Rattle & Hum* movie. Growing up, Brandon also enjoyed the Cars, especially the song "Just What I Needed."

His family moved back to Las Vegas, where he was a student at Chaparral High School. In high school, he heard David Bowie's "Changes" while driving with a friend down the Strip and decided he wanted to be a rock'n'roll star.

Teaching himself keyboards, he passed on college to take a job as a caddy at a private golf course, where he met another keyboard player. Together they formed a synth-pop band called Blush Response, named after a Vangelis (the *Blade Runner* composer) song. Brandon began writing and recording original tunes with his band. In 2001, Brandon's bandmates decided that L.A. was the best place to pursue a record deal and left Brandon in Las Vegas. None of Brandon's early songs have appeared on the internet yet. Curiously, no one in Vegas or L.A. has ever heard of Blush Response.

After being dumped by Blush Response, Brandon worked as a bellhop at Gold Coast Hotel & Casino in Las Vegas. "If I got a dollar every time I was propositioned up to some (sexy mother's) room, I'd be a rich man," Brandon has admitted. The bellhop job paid enough for him to buy CDs, a keyboard, and a 4-track tape recorder. He hated coffee, but he enjoyed a beer and a cigarette now and then. According to the *Las Vegas Review-Journal*, his parents have always supported his decision to become a rock singer, and were often the only people in the audience at the Killers' first performances in the band's early days.

It was when he saw U2 on the band's *Elevation* tour in 2001 that Brandon knew he was going to try to make it as a rock singer. He also had thoroughly relished an Oasis show. After answering a "Musicians Wanted" ad in the *Las Vegas Weekly*, he hit it off with his new bandmate, Dave Keuning, in late 2001. They recruited a rhythm section and named their band "The Killers" after an imaginary group pictured in a music video for New Order's song "Crystal." As soon as Brandon formed the band, he met his future wife-to-be, Tana.

"If I got a dollar every time I was propositioned up to some (sexy mother's) room, **I'd be a rich man.**"

Mark August Stoermer

was born June 28, 1977. He attended Chaparral High School in Las Vegas with Brandon, where he played trumpet in the jazz ensemble. Later he took music classes with drummer Ronnie Vannucci at University of Nevada, Las Vegas (UNLV). Prior to making it big with the Killers, Mark worked as a medical courier, shipping biohazardous materials and live organs for transplants from one end of the Vegas Valley to the other. This job gave him ample time to study the music of the Rolling Stones on his car stereo. Commenting on his medical courier job, Mark said, "It was a surreal moment, picking up Mike Tyson's blood-streaked piss for testing."

Mark doesn't smoke or drink, and both of his parents are doctors in Las Vegas. He loves orange juice and doesn't drink coffee. His girl-friend plays violin in a Las Vegas Irish punk cover band called Darby O'Gill & the Little People. Mark complains when his girlfriend irons his jeans. "I'm in a rock'n'roll band," he's explained to her. Before join-ing the Killers, he saw himself as a lead guitarist, not a bass player.

Mark lost a good friend and fellow musician, drummer Jason Rugaard, to thyroid cancer in 2003. The two of them had been band-mates in an earlier Las Vegas music project called The Negative Ponies that had achieved local success. The Killers performed at a memorial show in honor of Rugaard at the Palms Hotel-Casino a month before the band signed with Island Records.

"It was a surreal moment, picking up **Mike Tyson's blood-streaked piss** for testing."

Ronnie Vannucci Junior

was born Feb. 15, 1976, and attended both Clark and Western High Schools in Las Vegas. Later on, Mark and Ronnie would play in the UNLV marching band, on trumpet and snare respectively. As a kid, Ronnie claims to have banged on every object in his parents' house like a drum. He preferred this to hanging out with other kids.

"I'd lock myself in the garage and beat on the washer and dryer

and fridge - out in the garage - for hours on end," he told a Chicago paper. "I would do that in lieu of riding bikes with friends or something."

Ronnie and his family once lived on the outskirts of Las Vegas, but as the population there exploded, Ronnie increasingly found himself surrounded by more and more people, much to his dismay.

Ronnie is really the lone wolf of the group, a quality that Brandon most respects about Ronnie.

Ronnie has described his bartender dad as "a pretty weird dude, although he's calmed down some." It was through his father that Ronnie grew up listening to the Beatles, Steely Dan, and smooth jazz. He remembers the first cassette tape he bought: The Cure's *The Head on the Door*.

His parents bought his first drum kit from a heroin addict. Ronnie took to drumming right away, and began taking private lessons. At age 6, he became the youngest musician to perform in a Las Vegas band; he played drums for "Play That Funky Music White Boy" at a lounge in Caesars Palace. In fourth grade, he won his school's talent show for drumming. In junior high, Ronnie listened to punk rock and Britpop and wore white combat boots. He learned to play guitar from his dad after quitting the junior high school jazz ensemble over "creative differ-

ences." He listened to the Cure and Depeche Mode. In high school, he formed his first band, Purple Dirt. One of the band's members later went on to become Ronnie's dentist. Ronnie started teaching private lessons while drumming in a variety of bands that played everything and everywhere, from a desert show to a wedding.

Later, it was Ronnie who hit on the idea of sneaking the Killers into the Alta Ham Fine Arts Building on the University of Nevada, Las Vegas campus for practice. The band would rehearse in a soundproof rehearsal room from midnight until dawn. "If you pull the doors hard enough, they just open," Ronnie explained. "They make this big crack." After an all-night practice, the Killers would head off to their respective day jobs. Ronnie worked as a wedding photographer for, appropriately enough, the Little Chapel of the Flowers.

"I'd lock myself in the garage and **beat on the washer and dryer and fridge** – out in the garage – for hours on end."

Dave Brent Keuning

was born March 28, 1976 and is the most recent Las Vegas resident among the band. He graduated from Pella Community High School in Pella, Iowa. As one can imagine, there was not a whole lot to do in small-town Iowa. As a teenager, he blasted Aerosmith and AC/DC, and eventually he discovered U2, and listened constantly to the albums *The Unforgettable Fire* and *Achtung Baby*. Up until sixth grade, he walked in Pella's annual Tulip Time parade. He picked up the guitar and joined the Pella Community High School jazz band in Iowa. He also played guitar for a Christian rock band called Pickle from 1993-1997. He attended Kirkwood Community College and the University of Iowa, but eventually dropped out.

When Dave moved to Las Vegas in 2000, he suffered culture shock. "Being from Iowa, I can tell you that Vegas is not normal," Dave said. "It's cold on Mercury, but if you grew up on Mercury, that would be normal." Living in the Midwest, Dave felt he was the last one to hear new and exciting bands - which is one of the main reasons he moved to Las Vegas.

Dave got a job at a shoe store, but was laid off after 9/11. He used the time off to write music. "It was a blessing in disguise," he said. Eventually, he found work at a Banana Republic store in the Venetian Hotel-Casino on the Strip, where he enjoyed taking advantage of his employee discount. He felt it was a good job for him at the time because his manager was very flexible with Dave's schedule. Dave could take time off from work in order to play shows since the managers loved his can-do attitude and work ethic. He ended up working at Banana Republic for nearly two years. The salary was so low that Dave had to sneak into the Stratosphere Hotel-Casino and pose as a guest in order to wash his clothes.

Dave's favorite band is the atmospheric Icelandic experimental group, Sigur Rós. He griped to his bosses at Banana Republic that the Killers were always looking for a solid drummer (until they landed Ronnie). Dave wasn't wild about mainstream rock culture like Vegas radio station Mix 94.1-FM, which is ironic given that it's now the only radio station that plays the Killers' music in Las Vegas. Dave viewed the Killers as a mix between the Cure and Duran Duran.

As soon as he got to Vegas, Dave had placed "Musicians Wanted" ads in the town's alternative weekly newspapers, *Las Vegas CityLife* and *Las Vegas Weekly*. The ads ran for months, and Dave was beginning to lose hope. He presented himself as a guitarist with the stage name "Tavian Go," looking to start or join a band that was influenced by the Beatles, Beck, the Cure, Oasis, Smashing Pumpkins, and U2. Just before he threw in the towel on finding like-minded musicians, he received a call from Brandon, who had happened to attend both a U2 show and an Oasis concert.

Brandon sat down with Dave and they immediately composed a few songs. One, in particular, was about jealousy and violence, among other things. It had an ascending chorus that made Brandon happy. The song was called "Mr. Brightside." According to Dave, it's the only Killers' song that has been performed at every single concert.

"Being from Iowa, I can tell you that **Vegas is not normal.**"

Romance Fantasy at PT's Pub, Las Vegas, January 2002
From left: Ted Sablay, Ronnie Vannucci, Jarret Keene, Michael Valentine

FIRST KILLER

A Las Vegas anti-hero named Michael Valentine, immortalized, of course,

by Brandon Flowers in the song "The Ballad of Michael Valentine" first introduced me to one of the musicians destined to become a future Killer. While Flowers' song isn't exactly accurate in describing Valentine, it does capture the essence of the man. Valentine is a professional gambler based in Vegas whose own alt-rock band, Romance Fantasy, would inspire Brandon to achieve a new level of danger-ous romanticism in his songwriting.

Michael Valentine loves the classics of Western lit-erature: Jane Austen, Herman Melville, Charles Dickens. He's a huge fan of Roxy Music and the Smiths. He sings and plays guitar like Johnny Cash fronting Blur, and his band has played every Vegas dive bar from one end of town to the other. At night, you can find him at a poker table somewhere on the Strip, grinding out a few hundred dollars' worth of winnings in a couple of hours of play. Young women have been known to follow him around, drawn to his powerful 6'3" physique, his wit and charm.

At UNLV, Michael Valentine was a student in a liter-ature course I was teaching. One afternoon, after a class discussion about the music and lyrics of Nirvana's Kurt Cobain, Valentine expressed interest in my passion for alternative rock.

"I really dug what you were saying," he said, wear-ing sunglasses as usual. "You play music?"

After I admitted to playing bass as well as being a part-time college instructor, Michael Valentine insisted that I meet some of his friends, telling me, "I know the best drummer on the planet."

A week or two later, we drove to a house full of young musicians located on the edge of Las Vegas. It was hard to tell who lived there and who was merely passing through. The house was owned by the drummer, and it was remarkably clean considering that it contained a whole lot of twenty-

Michael Valentine

THE KILLERS | DESTINY IS CALLING ME

something Vegas musicians. That was the only thing remarkable about the house; it was a cookie-cutter suburban job chock-full of instruments and ugly carpeting.

The drummer seemed to be a nice enough guy - a laid-back, patient, and generous university student. His name was Ronnie Vannucci. He resembled actor Jason Lee, only less manic and much better-looking. He was a bit of a flirt, but harmless. It was clear that he knew a lot about music, particularly obscure indie rock, and he also had an extensive knowledge of classic rock, punk, country, emo, screamo, metal, rap, and classical. He also loved singer/songwriters like Tom Waits, Elvis Costello, and Leonard Cohen, which seemed unusual for a drummer. Often drummers can hate music with too many words but not Ronnie - he was different, literate. He had a quick wit. He wanted music to be fun, not forced.

Michael Valentine also introduced me to a multi-instrumentalist named Ted Sablay, a genius who could pick up any instrument and play it flaw-lessly. Ronnie and Ted lived in the house and pretty much behaved like normal college kids - except that they were obsessed with music. They ate a lot of junk food. They watched a lot of cable TV, sure - but they didn't play video games. It was as if holding a controller was somehow a waste of time. Clearly they preferred fondling instruments.

Valentine herded us into the garage crammed with P.A. systems, ampli-fiers, and various instruments, including timpani and a giant marimba. He urged us to work out a few of the original tunes I had written. After a few run-throughs, Ronnie wrinkled his nose and said, "That sounds like butt rock."

I was embarrassed. These guys were way out of my league. Rather than dwell on how bad my songs were, Michael Valentine introduced a new song he'd just written. It was a damn good song. Ronnie and Ted wrapped an arrangement around it with little effort. We were off and running.

Valentine announced that we would call ourselves Romance Fantasy. Ronnie laughed at this; it suited his goofy sense of humor. On the surface, Ronnie was a clown. Underneath, however, he was more serious than any of us realized. He was destined to be a rock-star drummer.

Romance Fantasy's first gig was at a PT's Pub near North Las Vegas's Nellis Air Force Base in the Fall of 2001. Valentine's brother, who performed under the moniker 'Danny Vegas', opened the show. (Danny Vegas would go on to open for the Killers in Houston, Texas. His signature song is called "Candy.") The bar was Redneck Central infiltrated by at least a couple of dozen hipsters. I worried that things wouldn't go well, but Valentine's bigger-than-life, urban-cowboy-tinged persona came across perfectly. And when we launched out of the gate with a retro-country rocker, the crowd really seemed to get into it.

That's when I first saw Ronnie come alive. He flailed at his drum kit like The Who's Keith Moon. During rehearsals, he'd always kept things under wraps. Now he was exploding on the drums, the showman revealed. This was the true Ronnie: a rock star waiting to happen.

But Romance Fantasy wasn't the band that would make Ronnie famous. The band played a few more bar gigs and even more house parties. In the course of a few months, we had gone absolutely nowhere. In fact, we seemed to be going backwards with a show arranged at Ronnie's brother's house. A nine o'clock show turned into a midnight show, and with an 8 a.m. college class to teach the next morning, I left and didn't look back. I'd had enough.

Ronnie taught me a hard lesson - that being in a successful rock band means never giving up on the band no matter how dismal things seem. Ronnie, for instance, had no qualms playing a house party. Ronnie would play anywhere, no matter what the circumstances. That's the difference between an amateur musician and a professional. This isn't to say that Ronnie and the Killers don't have egos. They do. It's just that they don't allow their egos to interfere with their primary mission: to write and perform heaping portions of tasty rock.

Romance Fantasy never invited me back; Michael Valentine remained cordial but distant. I still ran into Ronnie from time to time, and we ended up playing together again in an indie-rock band called Daphne Major. Valentine's band continued to play the occasional gig, but his job as a gambler held everything back. Ronnie knew this and bided his time, waiting for something better to come along.

Eventually it did.

DEMO-LITION MEN

Few bands emerge with a fully realized vision of what they want to sound like.

Typically, a rock group struggles to discover themselves through trial and error, using rehearsals to hone their identity. Not so with Brandon and Dave, and the two other musicians playing with them on bass and drums. (Ronnie and Mark weren't in the band yet.) They immediately created the signature song that would define the Killers.

alternative to the current scene.
—*Kari O'Conn*

The Killers
The Killers (three-song demo)
(Self released)

Normally, *CityLife* doesn't review demos. They are merely rough tasters of an artist's sound, and shouldn't be judged. However, the Killers' recent three-song sampler provides a great opportunity to talk about them, as they are one of the most intriguing new bands to kick up dust locally.

The Killers, thankfully, don't come across like any other band in town. The newbie act marries pop styles of British music with the lo-fi fuzz of modern indie rock, which is to say these guys don't listen to radio or even

"When I first met Brandon, he just came in and threw out some song ideas that he had and I really knew they were something special," Dave recalled.

In fact, the Killers' very first homemade demo CD contained three songs, one of which was "Mr. Brightside." The demo was recorded with a 4-track tape recorder in Dave's apartment in January 2002. One of the first people to hear it was Marco Brizuela, a store manager at Big B's CDs & Records in Las Vegas and a member of an indie-folk band called The Bleachers. Big B's, located next to the University of Nevada, Las Vegas, was where Brandon had purchased many CDs of the '80s alternative music that would shape him as a songwriter.

"Brandon used to come in here all the time," says Brizuela. "I remember convincing him to give the London Suede a try. He returned a week later absolutely gushing about the band."

Marco didn't get the Killers' first demo from Brandon, however. Marco's bandmate, Joe Maloney, had run into Tavian Go (aka Dave Keuning) at the Crown & Anchor Pub one night. Dave was visibly excited about the new band he was forming with Brandon Flowers and fetched a copy of the demo they'd been working on to give to Maloney. The two already knew each other because, at one point, Maloney had been approached by Brandon and Dave to join their new group.

very many local bands. This is exemplified in "Mr. Brightside," the band's best and most popular song, which leads off this demo. It's energetic, New Wave garage — a feel-good, Strokes-esque anthem that ranks as one of the best local tracks in a long time.

Odd, though, that the song hasn't received local radio airplay, and the other two on this demo have. However, "Under the Gun" — another catchy, retro-pop gem — and "Desperate" — an midtempo ballad that takes cues from Oasis, without the rip-off feel of peer act Psychic Radio — are welcome inclusions on what amounts to a sign of extremely promising things to come.

—*Mike Prevatt*

Later that same night, Maloney brought the disc over to Brizuela's house. They played it on the stereo and shrugged, unimpressed.

"I liked 'Mr. Brightside' a bit, but didn't think much of the other tracks," says Brizuela. "They sounded to me just like the Strokes and Oasis. If only I had kept that CD, I could have made a lot of money on eBay, I bet."

In the last week of March 2002, Dave Keuning felt confident enough to send out three copies of the Killers' demo CD to the three alternative weekly papers in town: *Las Vegas Mercury*, *Las Vegas Weekly*, and *Las Vegas CityLife*. Only *Las Vegas CityLife* opted to give the three-song effort some ink.

Earlier that same month, *CityLife* Arts & Entertainment Editor Mike Prevatt became the first Vegas music writer to notice the Killers. Tinoco's Bistro (at its old West Side location) had been hosting 18-and-up Britpop/Goth/Darkwave/Rock en Espanol nights on Saturdays called "The Ritual." On March 9th, Prevatt and about a hundred other folks showed up there at 1 a.m. as tunes by Tori Amos, the Smiths, and Boomtown Rats blasted in the main room, while Industrial and Darkwave blasted from a side room. But the evening wasn't all about vinyl. There was also a live band that night.

As soon as he stepped inside, Prevatt was greeted by Brandon Flowers, wearing a lot of makeup.

"He was nervous about approaching me," Prevatt recalls. "Brandon said this was one of his band's first shows, that he was interested to know what I thought of the Killers."

Prevatt hung around for the band's set, and enjoyed it. He didn't know the band's songs at the time, but later he would recall that the Killers performed "Mr. Brightside" and "Under the Gun."

In his March 14th music column called "Fear & Lounging," Prevatt wrote: "A live band, called The Killers, offered some melodic garage rock that sounded like The White Stripes gone New Wave; they play ['The Ritual'] periodically."

A couple of months later, the first music writer to tackle the band's music head-on was, again, Prevatt. "Normally, *CityLife* doesn't review demos," wrote Prevatt. "They are merely rough tasters of an artist's sound, and shouldn't be judged. However, the Killers' recent three-song sampler provides a great opportunity to talk about them, as they are one of the most intriguing new bands to kick up dust locally."

Prevatt, a huge proponent of electronic music, was one of the few music writers to instantly recognize the Killers' appeal:

The Killers, thankfully, don't come across like any other band in town. The newbie act marries pop styles of British music with the lo-fi fuzz of modern indie rock, which is to say that these guys don't listen to radio or even very many local bands. This is exemplified in "Mr. Brightside," the band's best and most popular song, which leads off this demo. It's energetic, New Wave garage - a feel-good, Strokes-esque anthem that ranks as one of the best local tracks in a long time.

Amazingly, listening to the demo version of "Mr. Brightside" today, very little difference is heard between the song in its original incarnation and its polished radio version. Everything is already in place: The incredible guitar refrain. The soaring chorus. The biting lyrics.

"The Killers, thankfully, don't come across like any other band in town."

Even the thumping drum beat. From the beginning, Brandon and Dave knew what sound they wanted to achieve, and they quickly made it happen.

The other two songs, "Under the Gun" (of which a punched-up version would later appear in the expanded version of *Hot Fuss* in 2005) and the ballad "Desperate", are less successful but that has more to do with their simple demo-quality arrangements than the songwriting itself. The hooks are definitely in effect, leaving one to wonder what might happen if the Killers revisited "Desperate" with a fresh approach. Chances are that song would be a hit, too.

Interestingly, Prevatt's review of the Killers demo appeared in *CityLife*'s Local Music issue, and the entire CD review page was dedicated to Vegas bands. Looking at these reviews, it's no wonder the Killers made such a splash in Prevatt's mind. The Killers shared the same page with an acoustic instrumental world-music jam band called The Reunion, a blues outfit called John Earl & the Boogieman Band (with their self-released album titled *Rib'n & Blues*), and an aging punk group called, appropriately enough, Aging Process. Given this context, making a splash in the wasteland of Vegas's music scene was not overwhelmingly difficult.

In any case, Prevatt and *CityLife* had provided the Killers with their first printed encouragement, giving them some confidence to take the next step: establishing themselves as a killer live band.

Icehouse Lounge, Las Vegas, June 2004

LIVE KILLERS

The band's first live performance

that really intrigued Ronnie Vannucci took place sometime in May of 2002, at a now-defunct all-ages club called Tremorz. (Ronnie has claimed to have first seen the Killers at a club called the Junkyard, but other Vegas scenesters remember otherwise.) Tremorz was located in a strip mall across from the University of Nevada, Las Vegas. The roof and the floor were both caved in, and the place had no amenities to speak of - just a barely functioning toilet and not enough $3 bottles of water to hydrate a single family, much less a few hundred teenagers. There was no sound system; bands had to bring their own P.A. system and equipment. There was no real lighting, just some fluorescent bulbs in the warped ceiling. The stage was maybe a foot high. Tremorz smelled funny; the funk of adolescence was powerful. In other words, it was the perfect spot for a novice Vegas band to cut its tender teeth.

The show was in bad shape from the beginning. There were all kinds of technical issues. Microphones and gear would suddenly cut out. Brandon had attempted to use an effect on his voice - some kind of tinny distortion - in order to sound like the singer from the Strokes. He couldn't get it right, though, and ended up sounding more like Cookie Monster than Julian Casablancas. The band struggled through the entire set.

THE KILLERS | DESTINY IS CALLING ME

Brandon was particularly off-key, uncomfortable and nervous, choosing to hide behind his keyboard instead of stepping out and interacting with the small audience. Being a frontman did not come naturally to Brandon.

In spite of the awkwardness and goof-ups, there were interesting moments. The Killers performed an extra-long retro '80s disco instrumental that started off corny, but gradually revealed a New Order-influenced melody that grabbed the attention of many of the Vegas alt-rockers in attendance, who made up most of the audience that night.

It was Daphne Major/Romance Fantasy drummer Ronnie Vannucci who expressed the most interest in the Killers. Daphne Major had opened for the Killers at Tremorz that night. When Brandon and his fledgling group hit the stage, Ronnie immediately took notice. He grooved on what he saw, obviously digging it.

After the Killers broke down their gear and began removing it from the stage,

Brandon was particularly off-key, uncomfortable, and nervous, choosing to hide behind his keyboard...

Ronnie asked his bandmates what they thought of the Killers. The response was that, buried under a tangle of glam-rock clichés, there were probably some halfway-decent songs in the set. But to revisit glam rock seemed silly in 2002. To the rest of Ronnie's band, the Killers seemed like a really cheesy Depeche Mode cover band.

"I actually like their songs," Ronnie was heard saying. "I think they're really good."

Clearly Ronnie saw something in the Killers that others could not, something that was invisible to the other musicians. But Ronnie didn't approach Brandon that night, most likely out of respect for the band's very young, inexperienced drummer, whom Ronnie knew he could smoke. After all, Ronnie was a classically trained percussionist earning a degree at UNLV, not a mere post-punk skinbeater. After that night, he got in touch with Brandon through a friend of a friend. The two maintained a close cell-phone relationship, especially after a Warner Bros. A&R guy named Braden Merrick contacted Brandon.

("A&R" stands for "Artists & Repertoire". The main function of a major record label A&R guy is to find and sign a recording contract with new bands.) Ronnie offered Brandon what little advice he could - "Don't sign anything right away, get a lawyer" - and encouragement.

Brandon, of course, knew that Ronnie was the best drummer in Las Vegas. If the Killers could garner enough attention from major label A&R scouts, Brandon believed he could convince Ronnie to join the band. Brandon and Ronnie shared a hunger to live the rock'n'roll dream. Not just to get laid, of course. (Brandon and Ronnie both had serious girlfriends whom they would soon marry.) It was simply that Brandon wanted to be Morrissey and Ronnie wanted to be... well, himself. An ambitious dream, sure. But Brandon and Dave and Ronnie had a quiet, assured confidence that would help them surpass obstacle after obstacle.

PRESS ON

Before Ronnie and Mark joined the Killers,

the band got yet another boost from *Las Vegas CityLife* and the unique Vegas music website, LVLocalMusicScene.com (now called YourLocalScene.com). The two media outlets teamed up regularly for "Band of Month" which would profile "an underexposed yet rising band." The story would run simultaneously in both forums with a big, fat photo of the band.

For the "Band of the Month" profile, *CityLife* writer Pj Perez met with the band at a Starbucks across from the university. They showed up looking like fairly normal kids minus any makeup and scarves. Pj had no idea he was talking with future rock stars. At best, he thought, they'll build up a little local following and fade away.

The first article devoted to the Killers appeared in the Aug. 8, 2002 issue of *Las Vegas CityLife*. Titled "Killer Buzz: Fresh songwriting and pop sensibility fuel The Killers' rise," the piece opens with a prophetic line: "The Killers came out of nowhere." From there, the article hammers home a backhanded compliment - that the Killers are a breath of fresh air, mainly due to the fact that everyone in town was still aping Papa Roach.

The Killers embraced the backhanded compliment in good humor, with Dave contributing statements like: "Even people who are into hip-hop are into our music. And some of the people who are into our music have come out of the woodwork, because there's no one else to see."

Rap fans digging The Killers? Imagine.

Unlike Dave, Brandon avoided pontificating on the Vegas music scene. Instead, he chimed in with only two sentences. Those sentences reveal a lot about the absolute determination that makes Brandon the star he is today: "Of course we want to get signed, make a record. I think we could make an awesome record right now."

He was right; The Killers could have easily made an awesome record in August of 2002. Unfortunately, it wasn't until two years later that the Killers would release a full-length album.

After the interview, the next step was to photograph them at a convenient time and place for the band and the photographer. After receiving a phone call which woke him up well after the crack of noon, Dave insisted on shooting the photos at a place called Mermaid Café, a cool little coffeeshop that dished up wonderful salads.

The shoot was scheduled for a Monday evening at the Mermaid. The band appeared wearing their well-known eye makeup, and wandered around the cafe like they'd never been there before. The Killers

"Even people who are into hip-hop are into our music. And some of the people who are into

our music have come out of the woodwork, **because there's no one else to see.**"

lounged on the sofas near the Mermaid's entrance and gazed around at the art on the walls.

The photographer, Bill Hughes, arrived late. The band had wanted to be shot lounging on red velvet couches, but Bill wasn't inspired by the Mermaid's furniture, and said as much. He lured the Killers outside, insisting that a photo of them in front of a man-made lake with the sunset in the background would make a compelling image. Brandon and Dave went for it.

Two years later, Island Records would shoot dozens of publicity images of the Killers lounging on red velvet couches. From the very beginning, the Killers had a clear sense of style and what imagery worked for them.

This early photo shoot of the Killers was interesting because it was the only one in which Brandon purposefully blurred the band's sexuality. He did this by reaching for then-drummer Buss Bradley's hand. Super-straight, macho agro-rock had dominated the Vegas scene for years. Sure, a lead singer or two had donned a skirt, but only as an ironic gesture meant to incite a wry chuckle. With Brandon, you never knew the truth. The makeup, the flamboyance... Was he straight, gay, bisexual? It was a mystery, and a mystery - as everyone knows - is an integral part of the mythmaking process. And Brandon was definitely constructing a myth. The "hand-holding" image accompanied the profile, the first spotlight in print ever devoted to the Killers.

Less than a week after the piece was published, Brandon fired their rhythm section and recruited Ronnie Vannucci. Brandon's affectionate gesture toward his bandmate, whom Brandon must have known he was going to fire in short order, was revealed as a sham, a Judas kiss of sorts. Brandon had used his outgoing drummer to transmit a subtle message about the band's ambiguous sexuality.

Another interpretation of this photo may be that Brandon is saying goodbye to the drummer who helped the Killers gain their footing in Vegas and draw major label interest. The gesture says, "Hey, thanks for everything, but it's time for us to take the band to the next level. No hard feelings; you're still my good friend." Indeed, in the wake of the band's massive success, many former members of The Killers continue to speak fondly of Brandon and Dave.

Who knows what was going on in Brandon's mind at the photo shoot that day? That's what makes Brandon such a compelling figure. Rarely does he reveal what he's thinking, but he clearly lets everyone know what he's doing. And what he does is write and perform incredible rock music.

THE KILLERS | DESTINY IS CALLING ME

UNLV Percussion Complex

BRINGING IT ALL BACK HOME

Sometime in August 2002,

the residents of Ronnie's musical commune of a house were shocked to learn that Ronnie had scheduled a rehearsal with the Killers in the garage. He quickly became the band's permanent drummer. The housemates were pretty annoyed. This meant yet another band - in addition to Daphne Major, Romance Fantasy, Faded Grey, and various other side projects - would be using Ronnie's garage for regular practice. Space was already tight.

"I remember kicking Dave's guitar pedals out of the way each time our band went in to rehearse," recalls one Vegas musician. "I was like, 'Get this going-nowhere '80s crap out of here!' "

Before Ronnie signed on full-time, the original Killers lineup performed one last time at Crown & Anchor Pub, where British expatriates in the Vegas Valley gathered to watch soccer. This show was even worse than the band's Tremorz debut. Like the Tremorz gig, Crown & Anchor Pub had no sound system, which meant no monitors. No monitors meant that the band couldn't hear each other or themselves, resulting in missed cues and flawed timing and all-around awfulness.

Realizing this, Brandon turned it into a comedic opportunity to entertain, and walked around the entire bar bumping into irritated boozers, many of whom simply wanted to drink in peace. Things got even uglier when the heavily-mascara'd Brandon fluffed his scarf and led his band through a miserable cover of Oasis's "Champagne Supernova."

The British ex-pats immediately booed the American band's pitiful attempt to pull off a legendary song by a

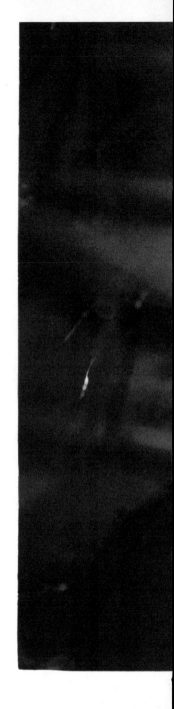

Ronnie's house was an odd environment, **mostly due to the musicians it housed.**

Ronnie Vanucci's former residence

renowned British alt-rock band. Indeed, violence seemed imminent. It was the first - but not the only - time friends of the band worried that the Killers might get themselves beaten up. Having been a Smiths fan in Nephi, Utah, Brandon was used to this kind of situation.

But the reaction wasn't entirely negative. A bartender was seen nodding his head to the hypnotic guitar line of "Mr. Brightside."

Ironically, hardly anyone British would boo the Killers less than two years later when the band took England by storm.

Now with the rehearsals moved from Dave's apartment to Ronnie's house, the Killers grew deadly serious. What was the band's secret to success? The Killers would beat something into the ground until it worked. Many songs took quite a few tries. Brandon would experiment with melodies and his voice at rehearsal. They simply played things over and over again until they got it right. And with the garage temperature always at a lethal 120° Fahrenheit, this was no easy task.

Ronnie's house was an odd environment, mostly due to the musicians it housed. At least they all had day jobs. There was Shay Mehrdad, the metalcore guitarist who designed and maintained the Vegas daily paper's website. Bronson Mack, a ska-punk growler who wore brown for United Parcel Service. Ann Yu, an indie-pop singer/songwriter who did everyone's taxes. Alex Stopa, an always-cheery Australian and college peer of Ronnie. And of course Ronnie, an alt-rock drummer who had fled to the academic environment of the university.

And then there were the musician friends who came in for practice or just to hang out: gambler Michael Valentine, trapped in a profession he never made; Jesse Harvel, the City of Las Vegas video tech who played a stinging lead guitar; and Ted Sablay, the hotel pedi-cab driver and college student who could pick up any instrument in the house no matter how arcane and play it beautifully.

This was the crème de la crème of the Vegas music scene. Everyone here was hungry for a record deal and super-talented, but nobody quite knew how to put it all together into a successful package. When Brandon and Dave stepped into Ronnie's house, they were stepping into one of the best collections of young musicians in the West. And they knew it.

But there was also a distinct aura of sadness about the place. This had a lot to do with the history of the Vegas music scene, in which alt-band after alt-band had had their respective shots at glory, only to fall short of any marginal success. In some cases, a Vegas band would sign with a major label, record an album, and the results would be permanently shelved due to a corporate merger, or the A&R person getting fired, or because the label had simply and suddenly lost faith in its artists. This left the crew at Ronnie's house feeling let down by the industry's superficiality and fickleness. At the same time, the lavish dinners paid for by record company execs - without a contract on the table at the end of the evening - had instilled just

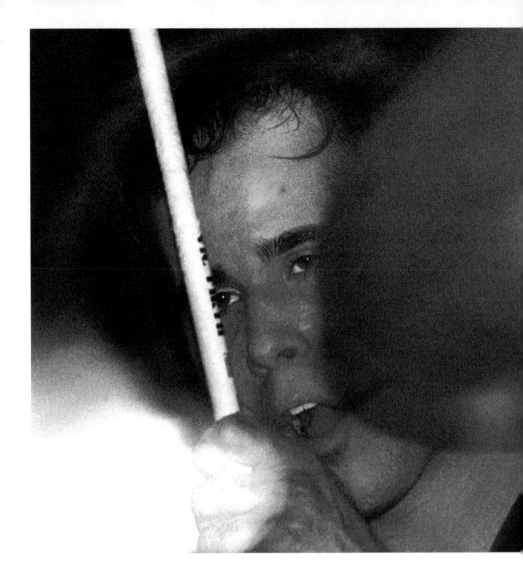

THE KILLERS | DESTINY IS CALLING ME

enough hope for everyone to keep chipping away at it, even if some of them were drawing ever nearer to age 30.

Ronnie's two previous bands, Attaboy Skip and Expert on October, had both come extremely close to signing big record deals. In both cases, negotiations had suddenly fallen apart due to a new trend (pop-punk, emo) that would send the A&R guys scurrying in a different direction, to a different genre, to a different part of the country.

Huntridge Theatre, Las Vegas, October 2003

ON THEIR WAY

Icehouse Lounge, Las Vegas, June 2004

THE KILLERS | DESTINY IS CALLING ME

Braden Merrick was a Warner Bros. A&R rep

who was always on the lookout for a new band that might make a lot of money. One day in August 2002, he checked out the Vegas music website, LVLocalMusicScene.com. He noticed the Band of the Month, the Killers, and listened to their demo tunes posted on the site. He immediately contacted them and took the band under his wing, giving Brandon and Dave advice, the first of which was that they replace their rhythm section immediately.

Brandon didn't waste any time. Besides, Ronnie had been waiting in the wings for nearly three months.

Braden wanted the Killers to sign a

THE KILLERS | DESTINY IS CALLING ME

contract with Warner Bros. Records and arranged showcases for the band to perform for label higher-ups. But the decision-makers weren't as impressed as Braden. The Killers were rejected more than once by the label. Braden never gave up. His own contractual relationship with Warner Bros. allowed him to serve as a band's manager, even if the band wasn't under contract to Warner Bros. He became the Killers' manager. A year later, the Killers signed their very first record deal with indie label Lizard King in Britain, after playing a series of shows in that country. The Killers' *Mr. Brightside* EP, put out by Lizard King in late summer 2003, sold out its limited first printing in less than a week, thanks to heaping praise courtesy of the British music press (*NME* magazine) and Radio 1, a major station in England.

How did this happen so quickly? The true story might never be known. Indeed, the Killers themselves have offered slightly contradictory explanations. But there are some puzzle pieces that complete at least part of the picture.

Corky Gainsford drummed in a San Francisco alt-rock band called Petrol. In 2001, Petrol signed a management deal with the Killers' future manager, Braden Merrick. When Corky got a well-paid gig drumming with Blue Man Group in Las Vegas, he left Petrol but still kept in touch with his old band and manager Braden. One day in January 2003, Braden e-mailed Corky to say he'd found a new band in Vegas.

"What do you know about the Killers?" Braden asked Corky.

Corky told him what any music critic and musician would have told him at that time: The Killers had some great, great songs, but not much in the way of stage presence, the singer was often off-key. Still, Braden was determined to check out the band.

Braden had been in contact with Brandon Flowers prior to January 2003, so it's not clear if this was the first time Braden had seen the Killers play live. Corky seems to think it was. In any case, Braden crashed at Corky's apartment a few days later. Corky and his old band Petrol scrambled to put together a show at the Junkyard with the Killers.

Darkness nearly engulfed the entire bar, with just a few stage lights illuminating the band. Like most Vegas rock shows that take place in dive bars, there was no sound system. The Killers played through their amplifiers; Brandon's vocals and Ronnie's kick

drum were the only thing coming out of a weak PA that might've been rented for the show.

Yet this was one of the band's first solid shows with its current lineup: Brandon, Dave, Mark, and Ronnie. The results were pretty stunning. Following the show, Braden signed on to be the Killers' manager.

Who is this person who brought the band from being a local Vegas band to an international sensation? From what people say, Braden Merrick is like any other artsy guy in his mid-30s from New York: fashion-conscious, trendy, always at the front of any scene. He's ten years older than the Killers and used to play in a San Francisco punk band in the '90s. Although he was officially a Warner Bros. suit, he was a scout: he didn't have the power to sign a band outright. Prior to Warner Bros., he worked for a website called RedButton.com, an A&R farming site much like mp3.com. He would bring acts to a label's attention and try to get a finder's fee. Braden excelled at getting tapes into the hands of important people in the music industry. Some people call him a genius. Others call him a music industry lightweight. Whoever he is, most Vegas music folks agree that Braden is primarily responsible for getting the Killers signed to Island Records. It is also rumored that Braden had a friend at Lizard King, which helped the Killers establish themselves in the U.K. These days, Braden Merrick has a management company, From the Future, that is once again looking for The Next Big Thing.

"I went from zero to hero," he says of his gold strike, the Killers.

Exactly what brought the Killers to major label Island Records' attention at the October 2003 CMJ music conference in New York remains unclear. Some people say it was Braden Merrick's industry connections. Others say it was the Killers' attorney, Robert Reynolds, who negotiated the deal with Island. What's confusing is how Reynolds would have the ability to carve out such a prestigious deal, given that he was a Vegas-based lawyer. Reynolds was a high school buddy of both Ronnie and Ted Sablay.

Ronnie had retained some of his record label contacts over the years, which helped to an uncertain extent in delivering a label scout to the door of the Killers - or at least to a battle of the bands sponsored by the alternative newsweekly, *Las Vegas Mercury*. More than one Vegas scenester recalls that Brandon had shared the prospect of Warner Bros.' interest with Ronnie. Ronnie, familiar with the boulevard of broken major-label dreams with previous Vegas acts Attaboy Skip and Expert on October, told Brandon to take it slow and not to sign anything. It's clear Ronnie was protective but hopeful for the Killers.

Merrick, of course, turned out to be the man who would take the Killers all the way to England and, ultimately, to the Grammys.

Prior the big U.K. push, however, there was the matter of finding a permanent bass player.

The Killers had some great, great songs, but **not much in the way of stage presence.**

Icehouse Lounge, Las Vegas, June 2004

KILLER BASS

Before bringing Mark Stoermer on board,

the Killers struggled to find a permanent bass player from August 2002 until January 2003. They spent the better part of late 2002 searching for exactly the right musician. By most accounts, Brandon, Dave, and Ronnie auditioned a slew of Vegas bass players, none of whom fit quite right. At least once, the band announced that they had settled on a bass player; and weeks later, the new bassist was replaced by another musician.

The musician whom Ronnie dreamed of enlisting was his housemate, Ted Sablay. Ted was the stone-cold genius of the Vegas scene who could grab the most obscure instrument and play it like he'd slept with it under his pillow for decades. Ted had cut his teeth with Ronnie in both the ska outfit, Attaboy Skip (in which Ted played guitar), and Expert on October (in which Ted played bass). Ronnie thought Ted was the perfect choice.

But Ted wasn't certain. First, he wasn't sure about the music. In 2002, there was no guarantee that the Killers would take off with their different retro-steeped style. If anything, pop-punk was moving more units in the rock genre than anything else. Even a celebrated '80s-influenced band like Interpol couldn't sell more than 700,000 copies of their debut album.

THE KILLERS | DESTINY IS CALLING ME

Enter Mark Stoermer:

Second, the record industry - as many rock musicians will tell you - is stacked against the recording artist, who must put him or herself in debt to a label in order to get an album recorded. Ted, too, was put off by industry suits who wined and dined and made promises to his previous bands, but ultimately didn't deliver. Braden Merrick did not, at first, seem so different. And even if the Killers signed with a major label, the chances of making a living as a touring rock band was slim.

Besides, Ted was busy working on his pre-med degree. Sure, he was a musical genius, but he also had an incredible scientific talent. In essence, Ted could do anything in the world. Why settle for performing in a band that would probably end up nowhere?

Enter Mark Stoermer: He was lead guitarist for a Vegas band, The Negative Ponies. He heard of the Killers' search for a bassist via Ronnie, whom Mark had known for years. Initially, he felt he was just a substitute, a temporary replacement, when he began playing with the band in October 2002. In recent interviews, Mark has claimed that he loved the Killers' music from the get-go. That's true.

But he also thought of himself as a guitarist and songwriter first, and a bassist second. He had his own means of artistic expression that he longed to fulfill. He shared with friends his concern that the Killers might not make it. His friends, to their credit, told him to hang in there. The Killers would surely get signed, they assured him. And they were dead right.

THE KILLERS | DESTINY IS CALLING ME

Café Espresso Roma, Las Vegas, February 2003

THE LAST DAYS OF ROMA

THE KILLERS | DESTINY IS CALLING ME

It's not an understatement

to say that Café Espresso Roma - located across from the University of Nevada, Las Vegas, on South Maryland Parkway - was the cultural and artistic epicenter of Las Vegas from 2001 until 2004. The coffeehouse was part of a West Coast chain founded in Berkeley, California, with additional locations in Boulder, Portland, San Pedro, and San Diego. The Vegas franchise had fallen into serious disrepair over the years (the espresso machine was more often broken than not) apparently due to corporate neglect and general entropy.

Competing coffeehouses - Starbucks and Coffee Bean & Tea Leaf - had moved in next door, essentially sealing the underground café's unhappy fate. But the university arts crowd was determined to make a go of keeping Roma open, even though they knew on a gut level that it would fail in the face of competition from more fully stocked, better staffed corporate coffee emporiums. The man who ran Roma during its final years was a part-time university student/part-time DJ named Ryan Pardey. Ryan, who was also Michael Valentine's younger brother, allowed the Killers to rehearse and perform after open-mic nights in the café. This was where Brandon and Dave (with Ronnie and Mark) worked out some of the material that would ultimately appear on *Hot Fuss*. Roma is obviously the source of inspiration for the song "Indie Rock & Roll."

Ryan gave the boys free reign over the place, sneaking them free coffee and sandwiches, letting them play in the empty café until well beyond midnight, particularly in the days after Ronnie had sold his house and before the Killers began stealing into the UNLV music building. (Understandably,

practicing at Roma was a lot better than being cramped together in the 120° heat of Ronnie's garage.)

Ryan also booked shows for the band at bars and clubs all over town, including Tramps, a drag queen bar on the edge of what was locally known with affection as "The Fruit Loop," a gay section of bars and clubs near McCarran Airport.

Brandon and Dave were grateful to Ryan. They returned the favor by appointing Ryan as their very first tour manager after the release of *Hot Fuss*. Later, after the band's touring schedule required a larger staff, Ryan was put in charge of merchandise - selling T-shirts and CDs at shows.

Letting a band like the Killers practice and perform at Roma struck many Vegas musicians as odd. Although Ryan spun a boatload of '80s alternative music in his DJ sets, he insisted on blasting pure indie rock on the café's sound system during regular operating hours. Walking into Roma, one was guaranteed to hear the tunes of a critically acclaimed artist or band: Modest Mouse, Elliott Smith, Flaming Lips. Occasionally, Ryan would crank some Weezer or Strokes, but for the most part, he avoided anything overtly pop.

Which is why plenty of heads were scratched when people heard that the Killers had set up shop at Roma. The music scene consensus was that the Killers were a retro-pop '80s band, not a bunch of indie rockers.

"They just **never seemed to fit in** at Roma."

"They just never seemed to fit in at Roma," says a Vegas musician. "I mean, they wore makeup and scarves and played a synthesizer instead of a glockenspiel, which is what, for instance, Death Cab for Cutie played on certain songs. Acoustic guitars were really big that year. A lot of us just thought that Duran Duran had invaded the place, and we didn't understand why Ryan liked them so much."

Ryan liked them so much because he, like music writer Prevatt before him, understood what the Killers were all about. The fact that they steered clear of the trappings of indie rock - a genre that Brandon felt had too many limitations - was what made the band stand out.

To Brandon, the world of indie rock was a little drab, transparent, and confining. He loved a lot of the music, of course, since it was obviously informed by the dark Britpop that had come before it. Artists like Elliott Smith, for instance, owed a debt of sorts to downbeat '80s alt-rock icons like the Smiths' frontman, Morrissey. But Brandon had no patience for the indie-rock clique.

A year later, when asked if being on a major label like Island was any fun, Brandon quipped, "They're a major label. It's their job to get as many people as possible to like and buy our music, and I am absolutely for that. I want as many people to listen to the songs as possible. We don't just want the hip, cool kids liking us. We're not afraid of people enjoying our songs."

Brandon has often mentioned his fondness for pop music over indie rock. "I understand a lot of the indie thing, but if you ask me what my favorite bands are, I'd say the Beatles and U2 and bands that were not indie bands."

I take my twist with a shout
A coffee shop with a cause,

then I'll freak you out.

"I understand a lot of the indie thing, but if you ask me what my favorite bands are, I'd say the Beatles and U2 and bands that were not indie bands."

As to his own pop tunes, Brandon has said, "We were shunned and made fun of [in Las Vegas] because we were obviously writing these big pop songs. And then it was like, 'What, so you want to sign to a major label? Do you want to be a corporate whore?' I can't stand that mentality, and I couldn't stand it even before I was in a band."

"In America, [indie artists] hide behind the fact that they are able to write a good pop song. They'll veer away from it right when you think it's about to get good just because they don't want it to be too obvious. We're all fans of big songs. I love hits."

Despite Brandon's desire to be loved by the masses, he still loved indie rock'n'roll so much that he wrote an ambivalent anthem about the genre. It's called "Indie Rock & Roll" and was included on the British version of *Hot Fuss*. It would eventually reach U.S. ears on the extended version of Hot Fuss in the summer of 2005. In the song, Brandon sings, "I take my twist with a shout / A coffee shop with a cause, then I'll freak you out."

Brandon seemed to believe in the indie-rock cause that Roma represented. He just wanted to freak the café-goers out. And he succeeded in doing just that.

Don Hill's, New York City, October 2004

THE DOTTED LINES

How did the Killers get signed to Lizard King Records, an independent

label start-up in the U.K.? According to many Vegas scenesters, when Warner Bros. turned down the Killers the first time, it was Braden Merrick's idea to market the band in Britain. After all, this path worked for Jimi Hendrix and many other now-legendary musicians. As you may recall, the story goes that Braden had a friend at Lizard King. That friend was Ben Durling.

Lizard King was started in 2002 by Martin Heath, former managing director of Arista U.K. The Killers were the second band signed by the young label. And it was the label's A&R scout, Ben Durling, who got the Killers on board.

"The first two songs I heard were 'Mr. Brightside' and 'Somebody Told Me,' " Durling told the U.K. magazine *Hotpress*, "and they weren't too dissimilar to what's on [*Hot Fuss*], so I thought it was a pretty obvious thing at the time. The whole '80s revival was starting to rear its head and the Killers were potentially a perfect fit. Bands like the Strokes and the White Stripes had also made it cool to be American again, so the timing felt really right. They have such strong, catchy songs and such great lyrics that everybody at the label was confident [they] would be successful."

According to Lizard King's Siona Ryan, the label signed the Killers on the strength of four numbers that the band had recorded with producer Jeff Salzman (who had previously worked with Green Day, Rancid, Offspring, Stephen Malkamus, and Will Oldham). Recorded at his studio in

Civic Auditorium, San Francisco, December 2004

"There wasn't a lot of production involved. It was almost like a live show or rehearsal. **No song was more than three takes.**"

Oakland, California, in March 2003, the four songs that got them signed were "Mr. Brightside," "Smile Like You Mean It," "Who Let You Go?" and "On Top." According to the Killers' then-manager Braden Merrick, the funding for this recording session came from Lizard King.

The Killers are quick to credit Salzman for the sound of their recordings, but they make it clear that the arrangements were their own.

"We constructed all the songs and mostly did everything ourselves," Ronnie told *Hotpress*. "There wasn't a lot of production involved. It was almost like a live show or rehearsal. No song was more than three takes." These songs and a few others produced by Salzman would ultimately end up on *Hot Fuss*.

After March, the band would not return to the studio until October of that year, just after signing with Island. This time the recording process and the ongoing touring didn't go without incident. Wildfires threatened the studio, which was located in California's Simi Valley, outside of Los Angeles. "[The fire] ended up catching up to the mountains," Brandon told *Pollstar*. "The ash was everywhere. We'd come out of the studio and the cars would have ash on them. We didn't have to evacuate the town or anything, but it actually got close." The wildfire burned 90,000 acres. Shortly thereafter, a sudden earthquake jolted Ronnie off his stool while he was recording a drum track.

But the band's manager, Braden Merrick, relayed to *Pollstar* the band's scariest moment in October. During a flight from Vegas to Houston, the plane in which the Killers were flying went into freefall for 1,000 feet. "A siren came on and [the plane] turned on its side," Braden said. "People were screaming and crying, and the band thought they were going down. They called me immediately when they landed and said, 'We're not flying anymore! That's it!' They've since changed their minds due to commitments, obviously." Reportedly, Brandon still isn't fond of flying.

Before the band signed with Island, the band was in the process of saying goodbye to Vegas. On July 14, 2003, the Killers played one of their last Vegas bar gigs at the Palapa Lounge inside the Palms Hotel-Casino. It was a memorial show for the Negative Ponies' drummer Jason Rugaard, with whom Mark had played guitar. It was an emotional moment for Mark and one that sealed his commitment to the Killers. His former bandmate was gone and so was his former band, the Negative Ponies. Mark had nowhere to go but forward with the Killers into a promising, if uncertain, future.

In the fall of 2003, Braden Merrick flew the Killers to England to push the *Mr. Brightside* EP, which contained the songs recorded with Salzman in March: the title track, "On Top," "Smile Like You Mean It," and "Who Let You Go." The Killers supported an indie band, British Sea Power, for a series of shows. The tour left an indelible impression on English music fans. The single "Mr. Brightside" was released in the U.K. on August 19th, and the EP hit record stores on September 22nd. It quickly sold out in both CD and vinyl formats.

Just prior to inking the deal with Island Records in 2003, the Killers performed at Tramps, the gay bar near the Vegas airport. Rumors were circulating about a possible appearance by legendary Def Jam co-founder and record producer Rick Rubin (among his gazillion hits are the Beastie Boys' *Licensed to Ill*, Run-DMC's *Raising Hell*, and the Red Hot Chili Peppers' *Blood Sugar Sex Magik*). If he had shown, there wouldn't have been any room for him, the place was so packed. And hot - there was no AC at all for this scorching September night. The sound, however, was incredible.

Killers ink killer deal

The local band that avoids press the way most other bands avoid things like, well, good songwriting and taste has graduated to the national level. After performing at an ASCAP showcase at **Don Hill's** on Oct. 22 during this year's **CMJ** conference in New York City, the **Killers** quickly signed to **Island Def Jam Records**. The deal, according to our sources, is the kit and caboodle and the largest in Las Vegas history: seven figures, multi-album, tour support and videos.

The band is legally represented by **Robert Reynolds** of the local Callister & Reynolds firm. Sources close to the band — **Brandon Flowers** (vocals), **David Keuning** aka Tavian Go (guitar), **Ronnie Vannucci** (drums) and **Mark Stoermer** (bass) — reveal that the boys have quit their minimum-wage jobs.

For more info on the Killers, check out their websites: www.thekillers.co.uk. and www.thekillersband.com. —*Jarret Keene*

Ap
Ste
rer
an
alb

t
a
o
Ga
King
getic v
Fooled
Brot

w

b
tha
har
ni

By this point, The Killers killed. I was at the show, and this is what I wrote in a review for *CityLife*:

> *Now the band plays the tightest, slickest, most vicious set of pop tunes I've heard in Las Vegas. The guys are even starting to resemble rock stars, what with Ronnie gasping for breath as he punishes his kit; Dave, his blowout 'fro in full effect, slashing and raking his guitar; and Brandon facing off with the front-row ladies as they touch his magnificent jacket. This much is clear: The Killers kick butt.*

The Killers performed at an ASCAP [American Society of Composers, Authors, and Publishers: an organization that collects royalties on behalf of musicians and songwriters] showcase at Don Hill's on October 22nd during the 2003 CMJ [originally the College Music Journal reporting college radio charts] conference in New York City. The Island Records deal was the kit and caboodle and the largest in Vegas rock music history: seven figures, multi-album, tour support, and videos. That month, the Killers quit their day jobs.

The band had at least eight tracks in the bag thanks to their recording sessions with Jeff Salzman. They only needed to record six more to put together a full-length album. Island suggested Alan Moulder to help produce more tracks and mix the album; Moulder had produced and mixed renowned acts including Nine Inch Nails, U2, and Smashing Pumpkins.

Listening to *Hot Fuss*, even the most jaded music fan can tell the results are pretty amazing.

By December, the band was back in England, gigging and working on pre-production for additional material that would appear on *Hot Fuss*.

Icehouse Lounge, Las Vegas, June 2004

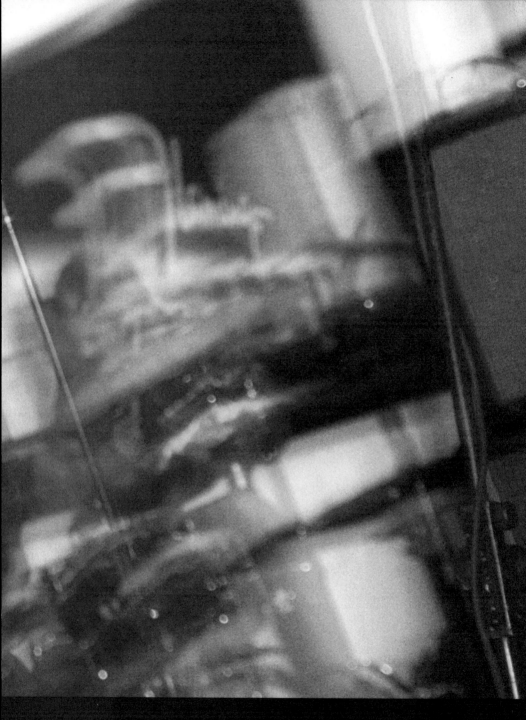

FRIENDS AND *NME*s

THE KILLERS | DESTINY IS CALLING ME

The Killers' rapid success in England arguably can be credited to one media outlet: *NME*.

The Killer's first U.K. *Hot Fuss* single on Island, "Somebody Told Me," was positively reviewed in the March 13, 2004, issue of the British music magazine. (The single's B-sides were "The Ballad of Michael Valentine" and "Under the Gun," a song that had appeared on Brandon and Dave's original 2002 demo CD.) An interview with the band appeared in the March 27th issue. And on the *NME* website, the video for "Somebody Told Me" could be streamed. The video was Brandon and the band getting their Duran Duran on in the Vegas desert. Nothing groundbreaking, but the song was so infectious that it gave the images a resonance they lacked on their own.

Even as The Killers made waves in the British press, the band prepared to launch itself at American audiences. But first the band played for an intimate gathering of friends, family, and industry folks at the Icehouse Lounge in downtown Vegas on February 25th. The event, thrown by *Alternative Press* magazine, also featured another Island band, a hardcore outfit from L.A. called the Bronx.

The Killers opened their set with the rousing dance-floor requiem, "Jenny Was a Friend of Mine" - and never let up. Highlights included "Andy, You're a Star" and "Mr. Brightside," that driving slab of New Wave-scarred disco. Ronnie Vannucci flailed at the kit like Keith Moon reincarnated. It was a memorable show.

That same month, The Killers were nominated for a Diesel-U-Music Award, part of a larger plan of marketing the band to a more mainstream audience. The Diesel clothing company accepted nominations by music-industry insiders (artists, managers, booking agents, journalists, label heads) in three categories (rock, hip-hop, and electronica). The Killers were selected as Diesel's rock band and were featured on the Diesel website and a CD sampler.

On top of this, the February 2004 issue of *Spin* spotlit Flowers and Co. as one of the 25 bands to watch for in 2004 - another feather in the band's cap. Also, the small write-up featured a pertinent bit of info: The working title for the Killers' full-length debut? *Hot Fuss*.

That spring, the Killers were on tour with Stellastar* and waiting for the June 15th U.S. release date for *Hot Fuss*. Ryan Pardey, Brandon's indie-rock pal from the Roma coffeeshop and Michael Valentine's brother, was appointed the band's tour manager. This was a highly successful tour, ensconcing the band in the alternative-rock scene and making a heartthrob out of Brandon Flowers. The day of the album's release, the Killers performed on ABC-TV's "Jimmy Kimmel LIVE." (Interestingly, Kimmel is a UNLV alumnus and a former DJ at UNLV's college radio station, KUNV 91.5-FM.)

The band also managed to play South by Southwest in Austin, Texas, one of the largest music conferences on the planet, in March 2004. *CityLife* columnist Joshua Ellis was there when ultra-hip comedian David Cross introduced the band. "I'd never heard the Killers before today," said Cross. "But now I'm a fan. I'll definitely be buying their album when it comes out."

Cross wasn't joking. Even the notoriously jaded Ellis was impressed. "The Killers are bona fide rock stars," he wrote in his March 24th column. "They sounded better than I've ever heard them. They even got a local Austin choir to sing with them [on the song "All These Things I've Done"], for God's sake. The two bands that followed them - the Von Bondies and the Hives - are far more famous, but sounded tired by comparison."

Also at SXSW, *Spin* magazine hosted a private party at a world-famous barbecue joint called Stubbs in Austin that would prove to be a golden opportunity for the Killers. The band played the party and less than a year later, they graced the February 2005 cover of *Spin*.

After their success at South by Southwest, in April 2004 the Killers rocked Coachella, an annual two-day music festival in the desert of Indio, California, that features performances by a variety of alternative rockers. That year, more than 160,000 people attended the festival.

"It is weird doing Coachella before we even have an album out," Mark told the *Las Vegas Review-Journal*, "but it's also an honor." By all accounts, the band triumphed.

It was a big summer for the Killers. They were handpicked to open for West Coast U.S. shows by the Pixies and Brandon's musical idol, Morrissey. The

band converted large crowds into fans in England at music festivals like Oxegen, an annual two-day Irish music festival held in July. In 2004, more than 60,000 music fans were in attendance. The Killers shared the bill with David Bowie, the Strokes, and the Darkness.

Additionally, "Somebody Told Me" was featured on an episode of the HBO series, "Six Feet Under" (Season Four, Episode Nine, original air date: August 15, 2004). The song reached No. 3 on MTV2's Top 20 Countdown. They also rocked the three-day Glastonbury Festival in England with every hot alt-rock band of that moment as well as legends like Paul McCartney. The band performed under the New Tent with bands like the Stills and Dogs Die in Hot Cars. In a *Spinal Tap* moment, The Killers lost guitarist Dave after doing some sightseeing on their way to perform at Glastonbury.

Brandon told Britain's BBC Radio 1, "We went to Stonehenge, which was the first time we'd been there. We've been here 14 times and we've never been to Stonehenge. Shortly afterwards we stopped at a gas station and we left Dave, our frizzy-haired guitar player there."

Flowers added, "It set us back three hours. We actually drove a whole hour without him and eventually he got hold of us. So we went back an hour. It was a big ordeal. I was watching *Caddyshack* so I didn't notice he wasn't there. He seemed to get through it OK. He usually throws fits but he did all right."

In September of 2004, the Killers got another boost when the band filmed an episode of "The O.C.", a hugely popular Fox-TV drama targeted at teenagers that reached an audience of millions. The Killers later con-

tributed the song "Smile Like You Mean It" to a subsequent "mix" CD released in conjunction with "The O.C."

Ronnie claimed he didn't even know what "The O.C." was. "We've been on the road too much to watch TV. If it was the Killers playing some birthday party at the Peach Pit, we wouldn't have done it. But it was written into the script that the Killers were playing at a club, which is what we already do. We don't want to compromise anything. We're not about to start doing Miller Genuine Draft commercials or anything."

The episode aired December 2nd. Seth Cohen from "The O.C." described the Killers thusly: "Awesome!"

Just before that, however, on October 6, 2004, the band played "The Late Show with David Letterman." And on November 11, 2004, the Killers played "Late Night with Conan O'Brien." They also managed to shoot the video for "Mr. Brightside" with director Sophie Muller, who had previously worked with Coldplay and No Doubt.

During this time, Brandon was already getting his first taste of serious fame. During a rare bit of R&R between touring legs he was back in Henderson, a city adjacent to Vegas. After enjoying a movie with friends at the Cinedome 12 movie theater on Boulder Highway, a female Killers fan was waiting for him in the lobby.

"Why are you in Henderson?" she asked. She had no idea the Killers were from Vegas.

In November, the Killers played a show in Ireland at Dublin's Olympia Theatre. Afterward, the Killers met Bono in the local renowned nightspot, Lillie's Bordello. "Spare us the interesting second album," the U2 singer advised Brandon.

In December of 2004, the Killers were nominated for three Grammy awards: Best Rock Song for "Somebody Told Me," Best Rock

Performance for Duo or Group with Vocal ("Somebody Told Me"), and Best Rock Album (*Hot Fuss*).

With news of the nominations, the band was in a state of shock - particularly Ronnie - according to *Las Vegas Review-Journal* columnist Spencer Patterson. The Killers' manager, Braden Merrick, phoned Ronnie's wife with the news. She told Ronnie as he was drying off in the shower. At first, he thought the band had only been nominated for one Grammy. When he heard three, he thought, "Oh my God! What have we ever done?"

"It's blowing my mind, man," he told the paper. "You grow up hearing about the Grammys, and you call your friends to watch the Grammys and they come over. That's the one night you don't do homework."

There wasn't much time to celebrate. After the announcement, the band flew to Portland for a show that same night. The next day the Killers were back in Vegas for the Billboard Music Awards. The boys sat with the crowd. From there, it was another West Coast leg, which wrapped up in San Francisco. The band immediately boarded a plane for a series of shows in Australia. The Killers ended 2004 with a December 30th performance at the House of Blues in Las Vegas, and a New Year's Eve performance at a dance-music festival in Los Angeles, where the Killers were the only rock band on the bill.

By the end of 2004, the Killers were too cool for rock school, leading *CityLife* scribe Jeff Inman to write:

The Killers. The Killers. The Killers. Everybody loves The Killers. Even God loves The Killers. The Dude is probably up there right now, his hair shaped like a "U," doing the pogo to "Mr. Brightside" while Jesus stands in the corner pissed because Dad won't listen to something more appropriate, like Michael W. Smith. That's how loved The Killers are: They make God be naughty.

Despite the cheekiness, Vegas music writers would never foment a backlash. After all, as Inman went on to say: "The Killers achieved the dream. They did what every Vegas band strives for: They topped Slaughter [the only successful Vegas rock band prior to The Killers]."

Yep, 2004 was a great year for the Killers.

But 2005 would bring even greater success. And a few rough patches that go along with being the most successful band of the moment.

Hard Rock Hotel & Casino, Las Vegas, November 2005

THE YEAR OF THE KILLER

THE KILLERS | DESTINY IS CALLING ME

Musical guests

on "Saturday Night Live" hosted by Topher Grace on January 15th. A performance during MTV's "Total Request Live" on January 18th. A performance during the 47th Annual Grammy Awards at Los Angeles Staples Center on February 13th. A stellar Live 8 set in London on July 2nd. An MTV Video Music Award and performance on August 28th in Miami, Florida to boost them into the recording tour.

You'd think everything was just hunky-dory for the Killers in 2005. Everything was... almost.

Despite the skyrocketing sales of *Hot Fuss* and the fact that just a short while ago Brandon Flowers was a bellhop at the Gold Coast, the Killers frontman found time to start a feud with the Bravery's Sam Endicott. It all started when Brandon noticed a slew of bands appearing out of nowhere and copying the Killers' style, replete with makeup and synthesizers. Apparently, Brandon doesn't believe in the old dictum that imitation is the sincerest form of flattery.

"Look at a band like the Bravery," he told *MTV News* in March. "They're signed because we're a band," Flowers said. "I've heard rumors about [members of] that band being in a different kind of band, and how do you defend that? If you say, 'My heart really belongs to what I'm doing now,' but you used to be in a ska band. I can see the Strokes play or Franz

Ferdinand play and it's real, and I haven't gotten that from the Bravery. I think people will see through them."

Brandon received a little egg on his face the following week when *Spin* reported that Ronnie had spent time in a ska band during the late '90s. Remember Ronnie's ska band, Attaboy Skip?

The Bravery's Endicott quickly returned fire in an interview on the San Francisco radio station, Live 105/KITS-FM, calling Flowers "a little girl" and "a kid in a wheelchair."

Then Endicott took a cheap shot at Mark: "There's the one guy who's like nine feet tall. He looks like a Dutch girl with a beard - but like a nine-foot-tall mutant radioactive Dutch girl."

The rivalry would continue on well into the summer. Surely it made for great talk at the water cooler and generated much publicity for both acts. *Hot Fuss* continued to climb the *Billboard* charts, spending all summer and fall in the Top 50.

Brandon's angst increased that same month when he announced that he didn't care for the "Smile Like You Mean It" video, which was shot in England. "Smile Like You Mean It" was the third single off *Hot Fuss* and was released May 2nd.

"It's very English-looking," he said. "It goes through the story of a house over a 20-year period of time. It's got a sentimental feel about it, but I don't really love the video, I'm really not too happy with it. But what can you do? I mean, they're releasing the song as a rock single, and it's the least-rocking song we have. It's a mid-tempo song."

Clearly, Brandon wanted more control over the Killers' presentation. Like any artist, he seemed to hate the fact that stardom and celebrity can undermine one's art. He attempted to reassert creative control by announcing a long-form music video in the tradition of Michael Jackson's "Thriller," only with more songs. *MTV News* described it as a "love-and-murder mini-story contained in two tracks ('Jenny Was a Friend of Mine' and 'Midnight Show'), plus one unreleased song ('Leave the Bourbon on the Shelf')."

Brandon being Brandon, he already knew what actor to cast for this project.

"I'd love to get James Spader to be in it, and we're trying to pin him down now. Basically, it's the tale of a girl leaving her boyfriend and him killing her and then getting caught," he explained. "To film it, we need a body of water, maybe [Las Vegas's] Lake Mead. We'd like to take the thing to Sundance or put it on a DVD or something. It's all a matter of time before we shoot it."

Indeed, Island had given the Killers the green light for the project. But as of early 2006, no video has appeared.

Adding to the pressures of making ambitious videos, stirring up bad blood with other bands, and dealing with a grueling tour schedule, Brandon was confronted with a lawsuit courtesy of his old drummer.

"This guy who was in my band a long time ago is trying to sue us," he sighed. "We wrote 'Mr. Brightside' a long, long time ago, when we had a different drummer. He had nothing to do with it, but his wife is a lawyer, so she just sent a letter to our lawyer. Wow. You always hear about people coming out of the woodwork once you get big, but this is ... wow."

Brandon obviously felt betrayed. That was the price of fame, of course: being the target of lawsuits. But he soldiered on, kicking off a new tour in April and selling hundreds of thousands of records worldwide. He and the Killers even added new songs to their set: "Where Is She," "Higher and Higher," "Daddy's Eyes," "It's Only Natural," and "Leave the Bourbon on the Shelf." This was to give fans a taste of what the band's sophomore album would sound like. And by May 2005, the lawsuit seemed to have gone away, thanks to the Killers' lawyer Robert Reynolds.

In June, another video was unveiled, this time for the gospel-powered "All These Things I've Done," which was directed by the acclaimed Anton Corbijn (who previously had directed music videos for Coldplay, U2, Depeche Mode, Metallica, and lots of other famous bands). It was a neo-Western that featured donkeys, sombreros, fake moustaches, revolvers, and deadly female assassins shot in grainy black and white. It made very little sense.

But that didn't faze Brandon. He was familiar with Corbijn's work for U2 and Depeche Mode. "And [Anton is] such a cool name when you're 12 or 13 years old," explained Brandon. "So he was someone we wanted to work with, and I can't believe we got him."

Regardless, the Killers couldn't offer a solid interpretation of the video, which was shot in the "Neon Boneyard," a three-acre site of historic neon signs rotting in the sun in downtown Las Vegas.

"The whole thing was [Corbijn's] idea, and there's still some things I don't understand," Dave admitted. "Like the donkey – I don't understand what that scene's about at all."

In July, the Killers played the famous alt-music festival, Lollapalooza, with the Pixies and Weezer. More importantly, the band performed at the Live 8 concert in London. Live 8 was a series of ten simultaneous rock concerts around the globe designed to raise awareness of poverty in the developing world.

"We're playing [Live 8] because it's a way for us to get involved with the issue without getting political," Brandon confessed to *MTV News*. "We're going to go up there as humans, not as the Killers. We want to go up and feel like we're responsible for helping people without getting all political. Once you get political, you're in a whole new area. And we're not there yet. I don't know if we ever will be."

In August, the Killers were added to the performance bill of the MTV Video Music Awards. "Mr. Brightside," featuring guest star Eric Roberts from ABC-TV's sitcom "Less Than Perfect," was nominated for four VMAs. Also that month, Brandon married his

"You always hear about people coming out of the woodwork once you get big, but this is ... wow."

longtime girlfriend, Tana, in an intimate wedding in Hawaii, which was attended by his bandmates. MTV dubbed Brandon's wife "Mrs. Brightside." Four days of Hawaiian surf and sun later, the band was back on tour.

At the start of September, the boys were back home, hanging out at the Beauty Bar and the Art Bar in downtown Vegas, going to a few parties thrown by friends. But by September's end, the Killers were embroiled in another feud, this time with labelmate Fall Out Boy, an emo band whose bassist Pete Wentz singled out Flowers on one of the band's message boards. Brandon, being the classy guy he is (and having had enough with the Bravery nonsense), refused to engage.

In October, the Killers headlined the inaugural New York City Across the Narrows festival (formerly called Across the Pond) with Beck, the Pixies, and Oasis, and joined Modest Mouse and the Arcade Fire for England's Download Festival which had migrated to San Francisco for some American action. But not before the Killers gave their hometown an explosive show at the Joint in the Hard Rock Hotel & Casino.

Indeed, 2005 was a banner year for the Killers, with two million records sold in the U.S. and another two million sold abroad. The band capped off the year by being named Spin's "Band of the Year." Brandon Flowers appeared alone on the January 2006 cover, perched on a throne and cradling a golden crown. The band was interviewed at length about everything from Jessica Simpson's bottom to the Antarctic documentary, *March of the Penguins*.

After non-stop touring throughout 2004 and 2005, the band is enjoying life off the road, though on January 5, 2006, at the huge CES (Consumer Electronics Show) convention in the Killers' Vegas hometown, MTV Networks joined Microsoft in a celebration at Pure, a nightclub in Caesar's Palace, to promote its new music service. Microsoft hired the Killers to perform. Amidst a wildly packed room full of computer geeks, even the world's richest man, Bill Gates, was rumored to be rocking out to "All The Things That I've Done."

SELECTED
DISCOGRAPHY

Untitled Demo CD
[Self-released, 2002]

1
Mr. Brightside
Flowers, Keuning

2
Desperate
Flowers, Keuning

3
Under the Gun
Flowers, Keuning

Somebody Told Me [U.S. Single, Island, 2004]

1
Somebody Told Me
Flowers, Keuning, Stoermer, Vannucci
3:19

2
The Ballad of Michael Valentine
Flowers, Keuning
3:51

3
Under the Gun
Flowers, Keuning
2:33

Hot Fuss [Island, June 15, 2004]

1
Jenny Was a Friend of Mine
Flowers, Keuning
4:04

2
Mr. Brightside
Flowers, Stoermer
3:42

3
Smile Like You Mean It
Flowers, Stoermer
3:54

4
Somebody Told Me
Flowers, Keuning, Stoermer, Vannucci
3:17

5
All These Things That I've Done
Flowers
5:01

6
Andy, You're a Star
Flowers
3:14

7
On Top
Flowers, Keuning, Stoermer, Vannucci
4:18

8
Change Your Mind
Flowers, Keuning
3:10

9
Believe Me Natalie
Flowers, Vannucci
5:06

10
Midnight Show
Flowers, Stoermer
4:02

11
Everything Will Be Alright
Flowers
5:45

Somebody Told Me Pt.2 [CD-Single Import, Universal/Island, September 7, 2004]

Hot Fuss [Enhanced Import, Universal, September 21, 2004]

1
Jenny Was a Friend of Mine

2
Mr. Brightside

3
Smile Like You Mean It

4
Somebody Told Me

5
All These Things That I've Done

6
Andy, You're a Star

7
On Top

8
Change Your Mind

9
Believe Me Natalie

10
Midnight Show

11
Everything Will Be Alright

12
Glamorous Indie Rock & Roll

13
Somebody Told Me [Video]

All These Things That I've Done [Import CD, Universe International, February 28, 2005]

1
Mr. Brightside

2
Somebody Told Me [Insider Remix]

3
Mr. Brightside [Jacques Lu Cont's Thin White Duke Mix]

4
Mr. Brightside [Original Version Video]

String Quartet Tribute to the Killers [Vitamin Records, April 19, 2005]

1
Jenny Was a Friend of Mine

2
Mr. Brightside

3
Smile Like You Mean It

4
Somebody Told Me

5
All These Things I've Done

6
Andy, You're a Star

7
On Top

8
Change Your Mind

9
Believe Me Natalie

10
Midnight Show

11
Everything Will Be All Right

12
Big Rig

Mr. Brightside, Pt. 1 [CD-single Enhanced Import Limited Edition, Universal International, May 10, 2005]

1
Mr. Brightside

2
Somebody Told Me [Josh Harris Remix]

3
Who Let You Go

4
Mr. Brightside [Video]

Hot Fuss [Limited Edition, Island, August 16, 2005]

1
Jenny Was a Friend of Mine
Flowers, Stoermer
4:04

8
Change Your Mind
Flowers, Keuning
3:12

2
Mr. Brightside
Flowers, Keuning
3:42

9
Believe Me Natalie
Flowers, Vannucci
5:05

3
Smile Like You Mean It
Flowers, Stoermer
3:54

10
Midnight Show
Flowers, Stoermer
4:03

4
Somebody Told Me
Flowers, Keuning, Stoermer, Vannucci
3:17

11
Everything Will Be Alright
Flowers
5:44

5
All These Things That I've Done
Flowers
5:01

12
Glamorous Indie Rock & Roll
Flowers, Keuning, Stoermer, Vannucci
4:16

6
Andy, You're a Star
Flowers
3:14

13
The Ballad of Michael Valentine
Flowers, Keuning
3:49

7
On Top
Flowers, Keuning, Stoermer, Vannucci
4:18

14
Under the Gun
Flowers, Keuning
2:33

The Killers sites

The Killers' official Island Records site
http://www.islandrecords.com/thekillers

The Killers' official U.K. Site
http://www.thekillers.co.uk

The Killers Fansite
http://www.thekillersfansite.com

The Killers Network
http://www.thekillersnetwork.com

The Killers Online
http://www.thekillersonline.net

7 Deadly Sins: A Killers Tribute
http://www.thekillers.stereooflies.com

About the author

Jarret Keene was born in 1973. He is author of the poetry collection *Monster Fashion* and editor of *The Underground Guide to Las Vegas*. Keene's indie-rock album *Die Kinder* is available for download at Mperia.com.